GERMAN BOMBERS over ENGLAND

A superb air-to-air shot of a Geschwader Stab He 111H–23 of KG 53, code A1 + DA. The three vertical stripes on the rudder are tactical markings. The individual aircraft letter 'D' is in green and the 'A' following it, which indicates a Geschwader Stab machine, is outlined in white (343/691/2).

GERMAN BOMBERS over ENGLAND

Bryan Philpott

**A selection of German wartime photographs
from the Bundesarchiv, Koblenz**

Patrick Stephens

First published 1978 in World War 2 Photo
Albums series
Second edition 1988

British Library Cataloguing in Publication Data

German bombers over England.—2nd ed.
  1. England. Air raids by Germany.
  Luftwaffe. 1940–1944. Illustrations
  I. Philpott, Bryan, *1936 –*
  940.54'21

  ISBN 1-85260-154-X

Cover illustrations
Front A Dornier Do 172 being serviced and
refuelled for another sortie.
Back A view through the nose of a Heinkel
He 111 on its way towards England.

*Patrick Stephens Limited is part of the
Thorsons Publishing Group, Wellingborough,
Northamptonshire, NN8 2RQ, England*

Printed in Great Britain by
Adlard & Son Limited,
Letchworth, Hertfordshire

10 9 8 7 6 5 4 3 2 1

CONTENTS

Acknowledgements
The author and publisher would like to express their sincere thanks to Dr Matthias Haupt and Herr Meinrad Nilges of the Bundesarchiv for their assistance, without which this book would have been impossible.

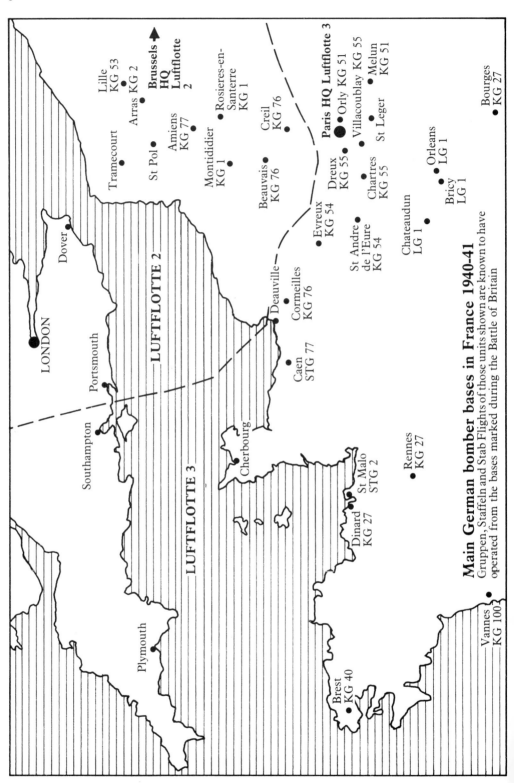

Main German bomber bases in France 1940-41

Gruppen, Staffeln and Stab Flights of those units shown are known to have operated from the bases marked during the Battle of Britain

Lille KG 53
Arras KG 2
Brussels HQ Luftflotte 2
Rosieres-en-Santerre KG 1
Tramecourt
St Pol
Amiens KG 77
Creil KG 76
Paris HQ Luftflotte 3
Orly KG 51
Villacoublay KG 55
Melun KG 51
St Leger
Bourges KG 27
Montdidier KG 1
Beauvais KG 76
Dreux KG 55
Chartres KG 55
Orleans LG 1
Evreux KG 54
Bricy LG 1
St Andre de l'Eure KG 54
Chateaudun LG 1

Dover
LUFTFLOTTE 2
Portsmouth
Deauville
Cormeilles KG 76
LONDON
Caen STG 77
Southampton
LUFTFLOTTE 3
Cherbourg
Rennes KG 27
Plymouth
St Malo STG 2
Dinard KG 27
Brest KG 40
Vannes KG 100

Within minutes of Prime Minister Neville Chamberlain's broadcast to the British public on September 3 1939, in which he announced that the country was at war with Germany, the warbling note of air-raid sirens sent people scurrying for the nearest shelters. Although this alarm turned out to be caused by nothing more sinister than a civilian French aircraft heading for Croydon, its effect on the public was not surprising, for during the previous decade most people had been led to believe that any future war would almost certainly start with massive air-raids. Several factors contributed to this very real fear of aerial bombardment: former Prime Minister Stanley Baldwin's statement in 1932 that there was no defence against the bomber which would always get through; the tonnage which the Luftwaffe could rain on British cities estimated by various politicians and political commentators; as well as somewhat exaggerated stories of the Luftwaffe's activities in the Spanish Civil War. But, as in many parallel situations, the truth was far from the fiction generated within political corridors and in people's minds.

The Treaty of Versailles, signed by Germany in 1919, placed severe restrictions on the build-up of military forces within that country. The army and navy were reduced in size and the flying corps banned altogether. Despite the restriction of engine size and weight placed on civil aircraft, the German aviation industry introduced many designs which, when closely examined, revealed their rather obvious military characteristics.

These aircraft were to be the backbone of the new Luftwaffe, but they would require crews to man them, and the training of personnel presented difficulties which were hard to overcome without raising the suspicions of watchful nations.

In 1923 the Defence Ministry (Reichswehr-Ministerium) signed an agreement with the Soviet government which provided training facilities at Lipezk for pilots, observers and air mechanics. When the new Luftwaffe was revealed to the world in 1935, the majority of its aircrew had been trained in Russia or through the Deutscher Luftsportverband (DLV), a pseudo sporting club.

Many of the crews who confidently boarded their aircraft for the early raids on the British Isles were experienced men. Some had flown with Lufthansa, some had combat experience with the Legion Condor in Spain, and others had accumulated many flying hours in private clubs.

Although casualties mounted throughout the Battle of Britain and the Night Blitz, Luftwaffe training schools were able to keep up a flow of trained personnel. By the beginning of 1944, the training schools had been forced to reduce their programmes drastically, resulting in pilots with only 100 hours flying time in their log books being posted to front-line units.

The Kampfgeschwadern did not suffer in this respect as much as their colleagues in the Jagdgeschwadern, but as training schools closed down, or reduced the length of their courses even more, many experienced bomber pilots were transferred to fighters.

Selection of aircrew and their training followed very similar lines to that used by the RAF and USAAF. The exception were observers, who in the Luftwaffe initially trained as pilots and received about 200 hours flying time during which they received their pilot's licence, before going on to their specialised training.

All aircrew spent six months in basic training, the emphasis being on drill, physical exercise and sport. Pilots carried out initial training at an elementary flying school where they were also taught aerodynamics, navigation, radio procedures, aviation law, and a host of other allied subjects. Successful completion of this course saw the tyro pilot move on to more advanced aircraft from which he would gain enough experience to receive his licence. Bomber pilots then went to another school where they completed a further 60-odd hours on more advanced aircraft, and from there to a specialist school to learn the art of instrument flying. The next stage of training brought all crew members together and they flew operational aircraft on simulated sorties until they were ready to join an operational unit.

During the early part of the war the observer was usually the aircraft captain but by mid-1942 this arrangement was being phased out and the policy used by other air forces of having the pilot as captain was generally adopted.

As pressures on training schools increased, the phases outlined above were cut down and by 1944 observers were receiving no pilot training and completing their instruction course within six months.

The usual composition of a bomber crew was pilot, observer, radio operator, flight engineer and specialist air gunner. The observer, radio operator and flight engineer also received gunnery training and manned the aircraft's defensive armament.

Pilots and observers were usually commissioned or carried senior NCO status, while other members could be almost any rank, the policy of having the lowest rank of Sergeant as in the RAF, not being adopted by the Luftwaffe.

Luftwaffe uniforms followed a standard pattern throughout the war, being field blue in colour. The familiar 'Eagle' emblem was carried on the right breast, this being in silver wire for officers and embroidered for Other Ranks. Flying badges were worn on the left breast and above them there was often a clasp awarded after a number of operations.

Shoulder straps denoting rank were in Luftwaffe blue with piping around the edges in Waffenfarbe; officers' badges were in silver fabric with piping and buttons in silver, and for NCOs the shoulder straps were in Luftwaffe blue with piping and a silver fabric edge.

Collar patches together with shoulder straps denoted rank, the background colour being the Waffenfarbe of the particular arm of service – golden yellow for aircrew – and wings, borders and oak leaves were in silver. A flight jacket was introduced into service in 1940 which was very similar to the modern-style battledress worn today.

Bomber crews often flew in one-piece light brown flying overalls on the sleeves of which were carried rank badges. In the early days of the war the life jacket was a heavy ribbed kapok-filled waistcoat, but later this was replaced by a much lighter inflatable type. Crews were also issued with flak helmets which were very similar to the infantry's 'coalscuttle' type but with wider brims to accommodate earphones.

On the outbreak of war the German Luftwaffe was not equipped to wage a strategic bombing campaign of the type the RAF and USAAF was to launch against Germany in 1943–44. Its bomber squadrons (Kampfgeschwader) were equipped with what were called long-range twin-engined bombers, but which with hindsight are better described as medium-range light bombers, more suitable to tactical roles. This, in fact, was their prime purpose as seen by Field Marshal Albert Kesselring, an army-trained officer who became the Luftwaffe's Chief of Staff in 1936. Together with Göring, he immediately cancelled the development of the four-engined Dornier Do 19 and Junkers Ju 89, in which his predecessor General Wever – a firm advocate of strategic bombing – had placed great faith. It is quite possible that if General Wever had not died in an air-crash in June 1936 the Luftwaffe may well have been equipped with a true four-engined strategic bomber by September 1939.

As it was, on September 3 1939, the Luftwaffe had on strength 1,270 twin-engined bombers capable of reaching England from German airfields. Of these 780 were Heinkel He 111s, 470 were Dornier Do 17s – mainly the Z variant – and 20 were the new Junkers Ju 88. In addition, there were some 280 Do 17 reconnaissance bombers and 335 Junkers Ju 87 dive-bombers; the latter being purely for tactical support of the army, which in Kesselring's opinion was the prime objective of the whole bomber force.

At this time Hitler did not intend a wide-scale bombardment of the British Isles as he still hoped that the two countries would not go to war with each other. If his intentions had been to mount an aerial campaign from German bases it is very unlikely that it would have achieved the rate of bombardment feared in England, since both the He 111 and Do 17 would have needed to have sacrificed at least half their designed bomb load if they were to carry sufficient fuel reserves to allow for variable weather, formation build-ups, and possible diversions.

The campaign in Poland saw the Luftwaffe perform its intended tactical role with frightening efficiency, which was again evident in the assaults on Norway, the Low Countries and France. Indeed, during these campaigns, with the possible exception of France in which RAF fighter squadrons were encountered for the first time, the Luftwaffe bomber force was virtually unopposed by modern fighters, and thus surrounded itself with an aura of invincibility.

The occupation of the Low Countries, followed by the collapse of France, made airfields available to the Luftwaffe, from which they could strike in strength at the British Isles. But military targets were still the main objective and deliberate bombing of the civilian population was expressly forbidden. In fact, in late 1939 and early 1940, the directives issued to bomber crews were very similar to those given to their opposite numbers in the RAF, insomuch as warships at sea, or in a harbour where bombs were unlikely to fall on land, were the primary objectives.

As early as October 16 1939 nine Ju 88A–1s of I/KG 30 set out from their base on the island of Sylt to bomb warships, including the Battle Cruiser HMS *Hood*, which had been reported in the Firth of Forth. The Ju 88s found the *Hood* in the harbour at Rosyth so were unable to attack it for fear of bombs hitting land targets. They therefore directed their attention to other ships in the Firth and scored hits on the cruiser *Southampton*, but lost two of their number to Spitfires of Nos 602 and 603 Squadrons. On the following day, four of KG 30's aircraft returned, again without success, but this time they managed to hit the island of Hoy; the first part of the British Isles to receive a German bomb in World War 2.

The opening months of 1940 saw similar actions around the coasts of Britain and especially in the English Channel where convoys and Royal Navy ships came under regular attacks of varying intensity. When it became apparent that the British Government had no intention of acceding to Hitler's requests and were prepared to fight on alone, a German invasion was planned and to the Luftwaffe fell the immediate task of destroying the RAF.

With Denmark, Norway, Holland, Belgium and Luxembourg in German hands by June 1940, the long-range Kampfgeschwadern could attack on two fronts, and those units based in northern France and Belgium were within 100 miles of major cities in the south of England. This meant that they could not only carry their full bomb loads but also operate with fighter protection.

The Luftwaffe was divided into Luftflotte (airfleets), each of which was basically a self-contained air force responsible for a geographical area. Within each Luftflotte there were two or three Fliegerdivision (later renamed Fliegerkorps) that usually operated with the Luftflotte to which they were subordinate, and in general terms each Fliegerdivision had a particular responsibility. Later in the war some special divisions were formed whose task was defined by their designation; hence a Jagdfliegerkorps was a unit comprised only of fighters.

In July 1940 Luftflotte 2 and 3, under the command of Generalfeldmarschall Albert Kesselring and Generalfeldmarschall Hugo Sperrle, respectively, were ranged along the Channel coast with a combined strength of 1,131 long-range bombers, while Luftflotte 5, under Generaloberst Hans-Jurgen Stumpff, could muster a force of 130 bombers from its bases in Norway.

Taken in their broadest context, the raids against British targets in the months up to July 1940 had been of a probing nature mainly against seaports ranging from Bristol to Grimsby and Hull to Liverpool. They did inflict some damage but not on the scale expected by the British Chiefs of Staff. Sporadic night raids in June caused more disruption of sleep by the widespread sounding of air-raid warnings across the whole country than they achieved in material damage. But they did prove the inadequacy of the British night fighter force, although, on the credit side, they led to the discovery of a radio beam which rumour had was being used to guide the bombers. As a result of papers found in crashed German bombers, British scientists led by Dr R. V. Jones discovered the existence of *Knickebein*, which was a guiding beam transmitted from within enemy-held territory and used to direct bombers over their targets. Rapid work by the scientists resulted in a suitable countermeasure in which a false beacon was used to confuse the German aircrew who had no way of telling whether they were tuned into the original beacon or the decoy.

In July 1940 the German General Staff made their plans for the invasion of Britain and to the Luftwaffe fell the tasks of (1) eliminating the RAF both in the air and on the ground, and (2) cutting off the supply of food and materials flooding into Britain via its seaports.

Back in December 1939 the RAF had learned the folly of attempting daylight raids with unescorted bombers – a lesson the USAAF was also to learn in costly fashion in 1943 – and the Luftwaffe were about to find this out themselves in the spring and summer of 1940. The task of destroying the RAF was planned to be accomplished in two ways, the first by tempting fighters into the air then engaging them with the Bf 109s of the Jagdgeschwadern, and the second by systematic daylight raids on RAF bases starting in the south and gradually spreading northwards.

The opening skirmishes in July were aimed at shipping and although these achieved some success they did not affect the determination of those manning the convoys to continue. These exchanges also probed the effectiveness of RAF Fighter Command, which on some occasions was able to take a fairly heavy toll of the raiders, but on others did not have sufficient warning to be in the right place at the right time. A typical example of this lack of advance warning occurred on July 4 when 33 Ju 87s of III/StG 51 struck at shipping and installations at Portland. As no RAF fighters were patrolling the area and none could be got there in time, the only casualty suffered by the dive-bombers was the loss of Leutnant Schwarze, who was shot down by anti-aircraft fire from HMS *Foyle Bank*. To the Luftwaffe commanders it looked as though perhaps once again the Ju 87 was going to prove a powerful weapon, but later events were to show otherwise.

Throughout the months of July, August and September 1940, a period which has generally become known as the Battle of Britain, the Luftwaffe strived to obtain the objectives it had been set. But it learned to its cost that tactics whereby fighters penetrated ahead of the bombers in an attempt to lure the RAF fighter squadrons into combat, thus giving the Kampfgeschwadern a relatively clear run, did not work. Although they had some idea of the existence of an early-warning system, the Luftwaffe staff did not fully understand how this operated, and broke off attacks against radar stations at a crucial (for the defenders) time. The Jagdgruppen were eventually ordered to fly close-support escort to the bombers, a situation which brought many problems, the most serious of which was the extremely short combat radius of the Bf 109. Another difficulty was the lack of communication between the German fighter pilots and the bomber crews, their radios not working on the same frequency precluding any form of communication once the aircraft were airborne. Without fighter escort the He 111s and Do 217s were extremely vulnerable,

their hand-operated defensive machine-guns being no match for the eight wing-mounted machine-guns of the Hurricanes and Spitfires.

On August 11 a large force of He 111s, Do 17s and Ju 88s escorted by Bf 109s and Bf 110s once again attacked Portland losing 11 of their number, but worse was to follow two days later when 20 bombers failed to return from 485 bomber sorties over England. Five of these were Do 17s of KG 2 which had mounted the day's first raids on the naval base at Sheerness and RAF Eastchurch, arriving without their promised escort of Bf 110s which due to bad weather had been recalled, the recall message not reaching the leader of KG 2.

The presence of escorting Bf 110s may not have had too great an influence, for by this time the Luftwaffe had found that the twin-engined heavy fighter was no match for the RAF's Hurricanes and Spitfires in air-to-air combat and required close escorts of its own! Another aircraft, which had wrought havoc in previous campaigns but now needed escorting by considerable numbers if it was to operate in safety, was the much-vaunted Ju 87. The dive-bomber proved to be most vulnerable, especially as it pulled out of its dive, and was easy 'meat' for the defending fighters. In the first two months of the 1940 campaign against England the Ju 87s were confined to attacks on shipping and harbours. However, in early August they were assigned to inland targets – mainly RAF airfields – and they began to fall from the skies like autumn leaves.

The toll of Ju 87s mounted and by August 13 the end was in sight when one Staffel of II/StG 2 lost six of their nine aircraft; five days later I, II, and III Gruppen of StG 77 lost 16 aircraft in attacks on the airfields at Thorney Island and Ford. Consequently, the Ju 87 was withdrawn from further operations against Britain. Three Gruppen were retained in France for possible shipping strikes and night attacks, but they were never seen again on daylight sorties where they were likely to encounter RAF fighters.

With the Bf 109s now tied to close-escort work their main objective in destroying Fighter Command in the air became more and more difficult. For a short while the tactic of luring the defenders into the air worked but this ploy was soon countered, and the single-seaters were very much tied to an escorting role.

Daylight bombing was proving extremely costly and on August 15 Luftflotte 5 attempted a raid on the north-east, their force comprising 65 He 111s from KG 26 and 50 Ju 88s from KG 30, escorted by Bf 110s of I/ZG 76. Sixteen bombers and seven Bf 110s fell to the guns of the RAF fighters in what was almost a repeat of the situation encountered by RAF Wellingtons in the Schillig Roads the previous December.

A turning point in the German offensive came on August 24 when the Luftwaffe accidentally bombed London, and almost immediately the civilian population was placed in the front line. A retaliatory raid by Bomber Command the next night on Berlin caused little material damage but contributed to a 'gloves-off' policy by the Luftwaffe and cleared the way for concentrated attacks on British cities, giving the RAF bases a welcome respite.

On September 7 London suffered its biggest assault so far when 372 bombers escorted by 642 fighters attacked the capital causing considerable damage to the East End, killing 448 civilians and injuring a further 1,337. Fighter Command, which initially was expecting the large force to continue its attacks on airfields, was badly placed at the start of the battle, but during the 90-minute raid they managed to retrieve the situation and took a heavy toll of enemy forces, especially when the escorting Bf 109s which were operating at their maximum range were forced to withdraw. That night a further 255 bomber sorties were mounted in the same area and the following morning shocked Londoners, some of whom had spent 12 hours in their air-raid shelters, saw the devastation aerial bombing could cause. But far from bringing a breakdown in morale, it only served to produce hidden reserves which increased the fortitude of those concerned. The German civilian population was to respond in a similar fashion when Bomber Command mounted their major offensive two and a half years later.

If further proof of the folly of daylight raids was needed it came on September 15 when the Luftwaffe lost 60 aircraft, an attrition rate that forced Operation Seelöwe (the invasion of Britain) to be postponed. So the Luftwaffe bomber squadrons had failed in their objectives, but analysis shows this not to be the fault of the crews but their leaders who at two crucial times changed their strategy when a policy of sticking to their prime objectives may well have brought victory. The switch from tactical targets, especially the Fighter Command airfields, to strategic ones came at a time when the RAF was almost defeated and, although many civilians suffered as a result of this, there can be little doubt that had this not occurred the course of history may well have been altered.

The Luftwaffe's change to night operations brought many problems to the defenders since radar-equipped night fighters were still in their infancy, and so for several months the Kampfgeschwadern were able to operate with comparative impunity. At the start of the offensive the units involved were still basically those which had operated with Luftflotten 2, 3 and 5, and these were brought back to strength with reserve aircraft held in Germany. The total bomber force available to Göring amounted to some 1,300 aircraft of which only half could be used at any one time due to the low serviceability rate.

From the night of September 7 the Luftwaffe mounted raids of varying intensity on London until November 14, a period of 67 nights during which an average of 200 bombers were over the city on each occasion. The size of each force was nothing like that mounted by the RAF against German cities, but it was for a longer continuous period of time. The bombing capacity of the Heinkels, Dorniers and Ju 88s used was nothing like that of the RAF's Lancasters, Halifaxes and Stirlings; nonetheless it was a terrifying experience for those who lived through it.

No 80 Group of the RAF had, to a certain extent, negated the Luftwaffe's guiding system *Knickebein* resulting in a large number of bombers failing to hit their primary targets. But the Luftwaffe had two other aids at their disposal, one being called *X-Gerät* and the other *Y-Gerät*. The first was operated by Heinkel He 111H–4s of KG 100 and consisted of a beam which at three points was intercepted by other beams. The first beam crossed the guiding one some 30 miles from the target allowing the pilot to set his aircraft up for the approach; the second at a distance of 12 miles and the third at three miles. Calculations using the aircraft's ground speed enabled the automatic bomb release to be activated on receipt of the third signal. This proved to be an efficient system but it could be jammed and eventually a suitable counter was developed. KG 100 acted as a pathfinder force using *X-Gerät* to drop incendiaries, thus illuminating the target for the main force. *Y-Gerät* was more sophisticated than *X-Gerät*, this time the release point being calculated by ground radar stations using an interrogation pulse against a response signal from the bomber. This equipment was used in He 111s of III/KG 26 and again became ineffective once a suitable counter measure had been worked out.

Although London had been the prime objective of the bombers other British ports and cities did not escape their attention, and on the night of November 15 1940 449 bombers guided by 13 He 111s of KG 100 dropped 400 tons of high explosives on Coventry, devastating most of the city centre and causing 1,350 casualties.

During the month, the Luftwaffe flew more than 6,000 sorties against British towns and cities during which they lost only eight aircraft to night fighters, although of course anti-aircraft guns and the balloon barrage accounted for others. Operations were curtailed by the weather in January 1941 but in February 1,200 bomber sorties were flown. The 'Night Blitz', as it became known, continued until May, by which time improved radar in new night fighters was beginning to take its toll. Although the first German bomber to be shot down by a radar-equipped night fighter was a Do 17 of KG 3, which fell to the guns of a Blenheim on July 23 1940, such successes had been few and far between and did not cause any great alarm to the Luftwaffe crews. The change in fortune is graphically illustrated by the fact that in January 1941 only three bombers fell to night fighters, whereas during May of the same year the tally rose to 96.

Throughout the rest of 1941 and into the spring of 1942 the Luftwaffe attempted no large-scale bombing raids against Britain, their efforts being mainly of a nuisance value often consisting of low-level strikes by fighter-bombers against coastal targets, although London and other areas did not escape scot-free. This method of attack was first used in the Battle of Britain and continued throughout the war. The damage caused by the small bombs carried by fighters – which came under the control of their respective Jagdgruppen – was insignificant but served to keep a disproportionate number of defending aircraft at operational readiness. The fighter-bombers would approach below the radar screen, then pull up to make their bombing runs before once

again diving below the screen to make their escape. The only suitable response was to mount standing patrols, since any fighter scrambled to intercept had no hope of catching the intruder before it had dropped its load.

Incensed by Bomber Command's attacks on German cities, especially the one against Lübeck on March 28 1942, Hitler ordered a new series of attacks which have become known as the 'Baedecker' raids. These began on April 23 when Do 217s of KG 2 and Ju 88s of KG 106, led by a small force of He 111s of I/KG 100, bombed Exeter. The following night the same target was attacked twice and on the 25th the ancient city of Bath received the attention of 151 bombers in two raids. The pattern of these attacks gradually emerged as being of short duration against lightly defended targets, mainly carried out on bright moonlight nights. The new Beaufighter and Mosquito night fighters took a steady toll of the raiders and, although Hull, Grimsby, Southampton, Bristol, Norwich, Birmingham, Ipswich and Canterbury, featured among the targets, damage and casualties were not nearly as great as they had been during the Night Blitz. Another feature of the raids in 1942 was the use of special high-altitude Ju 86 bombers but they were never available in a quantity likely to cause embarrassment to the defenders. The last major raid of 1942 came in October and was mounted by FW 190 fighter-bombers against Canterbury. This resulted in 28 bombs hitting various parts of the city, but the raid and the night attack which followed caused only 87 casualties.

In January 1943 KG 2 and KG 6, now equipped with the latest versions of the Do 217 and Ju 88, mounted a raid of 118 aircraft on the night of the 17th against London, and on the 20th fighter-bombers visited the capital at dusk. This pattern of mixed attacks in various strengths continued throughout the year but by now the fighter defence with its AI radar was honed to a fine degree and the night skies over England were no place for the German bomber crews to be. The fighter-bombers, however, also operated at night and their speed made them an entirely different proposition, very few of them falling to the guns of defending night fighters.

Although these raids were small in terms of aircraft involved and never lasted long they were intense inasmuch as some targets were visited twice a night, often the same bomber crews flying both missions. Therefore they managed to keep a very high proportion of manpower tied down on defence, as well as providing useful propaganda for the beleagured German civilian population.

The losses suffered by the German bomber force in 1943 were severe when compared to its total strength and results achieved. However, in December Göring came under increasing pressure to mount further retaliatory raids against England in greater strength. The only way he could do this was to withdraw units from other fronts. This took time and the starting date for Operation Steinbock, as it was called, continued to be delayed. By the end of January 1944 the force was ready. Although the main equipment still comprised basically improved versions of the twins which had borne the brunt of the German bombing efforts since 1940, there were new aircraft in the form of the Ju 188 and He 177, the latter a heavy bomber with four engines ganged in pairs which was dogged by problems throughout its inauspicious career.

On the night of January 21 a force of 227 bombers set out to attack London. The use of Düppel, the German equivalent to Window, confused the defenders' radar, and Ju 88 and 188 aircraft guided the force in by dropping markers. The raiders returned to their bases after bombing, where they were quickly refuelled and soon airborne, once again heading to London. The two raids caused very little damage and ten per cent of the raiding force was lost, a rate which could not be sustained. Further attacks on London in January, March and April were mounted as were sorties against other cities. But by May more than 60 per cent of the bomber force which had been available at the start of Operation Steinbock had been lost. Although these could be replaced by new aircraft, trained crews were just not available, and to throw partly trained crews into the cauldron over England had already proved disastrous during the 'mini Blitz' of 1943 when heavy losses were incurred.

In June 1944 the Allies invaded Europe and gradually forward bomber bases were overrun and thus denied to the Luftwaffe. For the rest of the war manned German bomber sorties against England were practically non-existent but the unmanned V1 continued to harass the population until their bases were destroyed in the Allied advance. Some of the unmanned missiles were launched by adapted He 111s, and He 177s were also used to launch guided bombs, but British air superiority was such that by this time even 'stand-off' operations of this nature were fraught with danger.

The last ace to be played by the Germans was the V2 rocket, against which there was no defence, but this was operated by the German army so cannot be covered in this brief résumé of Luftwaffe bomber operations.

By May 1945 the once-proud Kampfgeschwadern of the Luftwaffe had been all but wiped out. The gallant crews had set out in 1940 to prepare the way for a victorious invasion by the German army, but they had met a force more resolute and better equipped than any they had previously encountered. Also, when they switched from a tactical to a strategic role, they had neither the aircraft nor the ability to succeed.

During the Luftwaffe bomber campaign against Britain 60,500 civilians were killed and 85,000 injured, the majority of these casualties – some 50,000 – occurring during the Blitz of 1940. As sad as these figures are they represent only a small proportion of those suffered by the German civilian population during the strategic bomber offensive mounted by the RAF and USAAF in 1943 to 1945. In both cases neither bomber force achieved the breakdown in civilian morale which had been widely forecast in pre-war days as being one of the certainties of a large-scale bomber offensive.

The photographs in this book have been selected with care from the Bundesarchiv, Koblenz (the approximate German equivalent of the US National Archives or the British Public Records Office). Particular attention has been devoted to choosing photographs which will be fresh to the majority of readers, although it is inevitable that one or two may be familiar. Other than this, the author's prime concern has been to choose good-quality photographs which illustrate the type of detail that enthusiasts and modellers require. In certain instances quality has, to a degree, been sacrificed in order to include a particularly interesting photograph. For the most part, however, the quality speaks for itself.

The Bundesarchiv files hold some one million black and white negatives of Wehrmacht and Luftwaffe subjects, including 150,000 on the Kriegsmarine, some 20,000 glass negatives from the inter-war period and several hundred colour photographs. Sheer numbers is one of the problems which makes the compilation of a book such as this difficult. Other difficulties include the fact that, in the vast majority of cases, the negatives have not been printed so the researcher is forced to look through boxes of 35 mm contact strips – some 250 boxes containing an average of over 5,000 pictures each, plus folders containing a further 115,000 contact prints of the Waffen-SS; moreover, cataloguing and indexing the negatives is neither an easy nor a short task, with the result that, at the present time, Luftwaffe and Wehrmacht subjects as well as entirely separate theatres of operations are intermingled in the same files.

There is a simple explanation for this confusion. The Bundesarchiv photographs were taken by war correspondents attached to German military units, and the negatives were originally stored in the Reich Propaganda Ministry in Berlin. Towards the close of World War 2, all the photographs – then numbering some $3\frac{1}{2}$ million – were ordered to be destroyed. One man in the Ministry, a Herr Evers, realised that they should be preserved for posterity and, acting entirely unofficially and on his own initiative, commandeered the first available suitable transport – two refrigerated fish trucks – loaded the negatives into them, and set out for safety. Unfortunately, one of the trucks disappeared en route and, to this day, nobody knows what happened to it. The remainder were captured by the Americans and shipped to Washington, where they remained for 20 years before the majority were returned to the government of West Germany. A large number, however, still reside in Washington. Thus the Bundesarchiv files are incomplete, with infuriating gaps for any researcher. Specifically, they end in the autumn of 1944, after Arnhem, and thus record none of the drama of the closing months of the war.

The photographs are currently housed in a modern office block in Koblenz, overlooking the River Mosel. The priceless negatives are stored in the basement, and there are strict security checks on anyone seeking admission to the Bildarchiv (Photo Archive). Regrettably, and the author has been asked to stress this point, the archives are *only open to bona fide authors and publishers, and prints can only be supplied for reproduction in a book or magazine*. They CANNOT be supplied to private collectors or enthusiasts for personal use, so *please* – don't write to the Bundesarchiv or the publishers of this book asking for copy prints, because they cannot be provided. The well-equipped photo laboratory at the Bundesarchiv is only capable of handling some 80 to 100 prints per day because each is printed individually under strictly controlled conditions – another reason for the fine quality of the photographs but also a contributory factor in the above legislation.

THE PHOTOGRAPHS

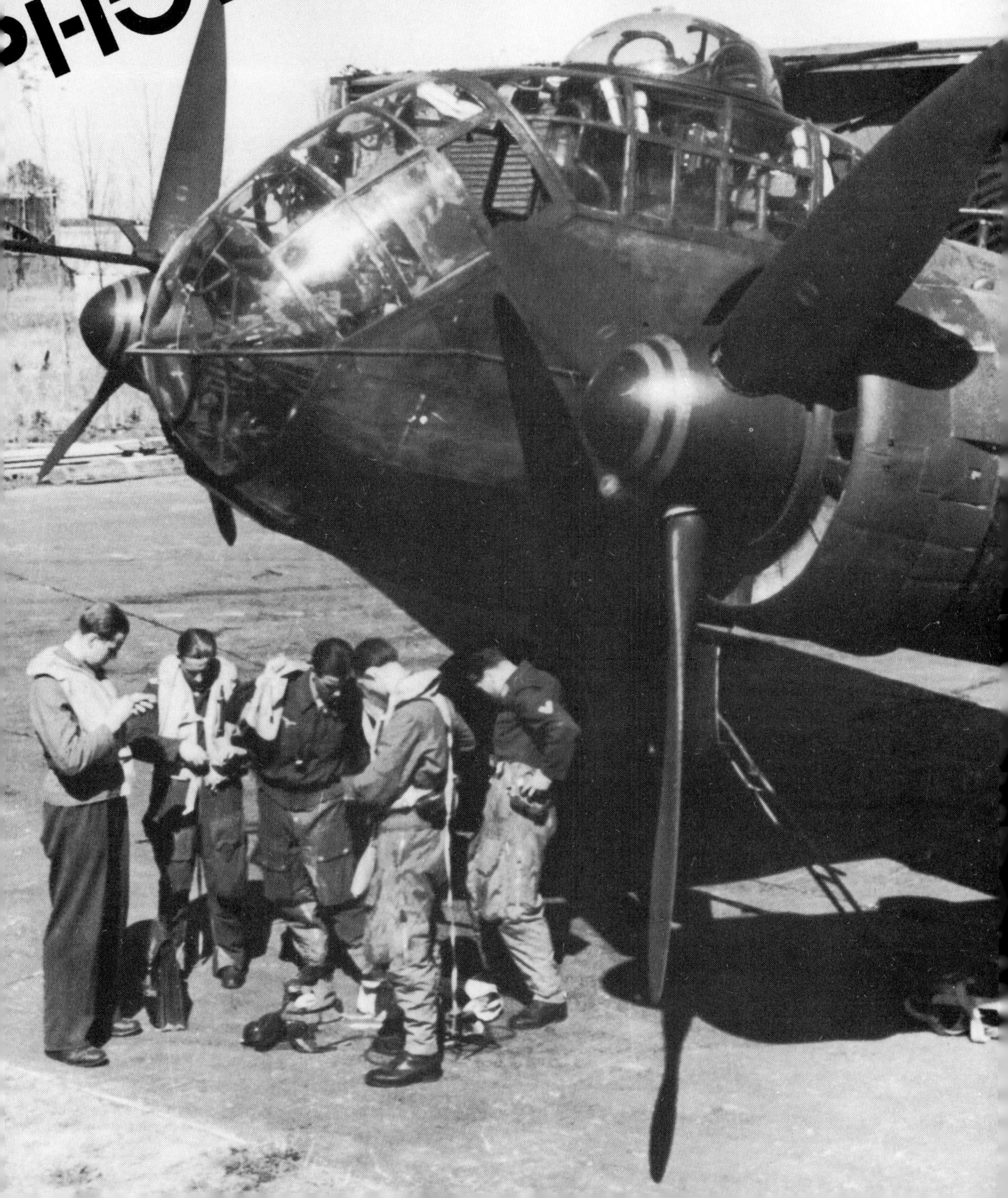

Previous page A Ju 188A–2 clearly showing the turret-mounted MG 151. This particular bomber was used to attack Allied forces at Arnhem in September 1944, as well as taking part in the 1944 Night Blitz over England (497/352/20).

Inset left The men who painted the badges are not often seen at work, and this one appears to have an oversized paintbrush for the delicate work he is doing on a He 111 of an unknown unit. Camouflage is 70/71/65 (317/32/1).

Inset right These are very early He 111Bs of KG 26, probably III Gruppe aircraft, and show the unit's famous 'Lion' badge to advantage (76/99/28a).

Background photograph The He 111 formed the backbone of the Luftwaffe's bomber units during the first campaign against England. This example is a Geschwader Stab aircraft of KG 26, 1H + DA, the individual aircraft letter 'D' being in green (604/1513/31).

Supporting the He 111 in some quantity was the Do 17Z–2 known as the 'flying pencil'. This aircraft, 5K + FA, is a Geschwader Stab machine of KG 3 and carries the red/white shield badge of the City of Elbing on its nose (343/679/14A).

A Do 17Z–2 of KG 3, probably at Le Culot, Belgium, 1940. The badge is the emblem of the City of Elbing and has a red cross on a white background in the top half and the colours reversed in the bottom. The open entry hatch and stencilling are worth noting by modellers (345/784/11).

The infamous Ju 87 Stuka met its Waterloo against the RAF and after severe punishment was withdrawn. These two are Ju 87B–1s of StG 51, the nearest being 6G + GB, the 'B' indicating it is a I Gruppe Stab aircraft (378/43/30).

Operating with KG 30 was the Ju 88A–1 which was to see life in many roles during the war. This example is from the 5th Staffel of II/KG 30. In this case the badge has a white background with red top corner and yellow bottom corner, the diving bird being black. In some cases the background colour of the shield was one colour only; white for I Gruppe, red for II and yellow for III (426/376/35a).

Above Very good profile view of He 111s flying in a standard Luftwaffe formation. The mixture of markings, including simplified cross on photographic aircraft, outlined swastika on nearest machine and early style fuselage crosses, is of great interest (76/99/31).

Above right Badge of KG 55 painted on the nose of an He 111 in France, 1940 (340/183/25).

Right A Ju 88A–1 of I/KG 54 which crashed near Dieppe on August 28 1940. The original caption to this photograph when it appeared in German newspapers claimed that it showed Luftwaffe officers inspecting the wreck of a crashed RAF bomber! (71/60/59).

Above left Formation of He 111Hs crossing the English coastline. It was believed that the combined cross-fire from this type of formation would produce enough defence to deter fighter attack (72/85/35).

Left The excellent view from the pilot's position of the He 111 is very apparent in this view of a formation from an unknown unit (72/85/28).

Above Do 17Z–2s of 9/KG 76 flown by Unteroffizier Massen, Oberleutnant Lamberti and Feldwebel Raab at low level near Beachy Head and the Seven Sisters, *en route* to attacking RAF Kenley on August 18 1940 (385/563/11a).

Above left Sizing up the opposition. Luftwaffe personnel inspect a Handley Page Hampden of No 61 Squadron in France. The Hampden was a contemporary of the He 111 and Do 17 (341/492/38).

Left Two Luftwaffe ground crew, known as 'black men', inspect battle damage on an He 111H of 4/KG 1 (*Hindenburg*) after a sortie over England during August 1940 (385/570/9).

Above right A No 64 Squadron Spitfire can be seen in its protected dispersal as Do 17Z–2s of 9/KG 76 bomb Kenley on August 18 1940 (385/563/18a).

Right Part of the Seven Sisters photographed by Rolf von Pebal from a Do 17 of 9/KG 76, flown by Feldwebel Reichel, returning from the August 18 raid (385/563/24).

Inset above A1 + JN of the 5th Staffel, II/KG 53, airborne from Lille-Nord, France, in 1940 (343/695/10).

Inset above left Badges often depicted the function of the unit concerned, and in this case the connection between the telescope and a reconnaissance unit is obvious. The aircraft is a Do 17P of Auf K1 Gr 123 (340/159/6a).

Inset left Ikaria flexible mounting for the nose 7·9 mm MG 15 machine-gun of a He 111 (499/60/14).

Background photograph He 111H of 9/KG 53 which suffered a port undercarriage collapse on landing at Villacoublay in 1940. Aircraft code is A1+ DT and the white bands which can be seen on the top of the starboard wing are tactical markings indicating a III Gruppe aircraft, used during the Battle of Britain and the first night Blitz (343/695/17).

Inset above An Obergefreiter despatch rider collects a film cassette from the pilot of a KG 53 He 111 in Belgium. The aircraft carries only the letter 'J' behind the fuselage cross but there is evidence of other markings having been painted out (344/733/22).

Above Ju 88A–1 of KG 30 preparing for take-off. The diving eagle badge had its background colours painted in the appropriate Staffel colours, see also photo 426/376/35a on page 19 (344/744/9a).

Above left Dorsal gunner of an He 111 clearly showing the hand-swivelled 7·9 mm MG 15 machine-gun and its ring and bead sight. The gunner is wearing a light brown one-piece flying suit and an inflatable life jacket whose mouthpiece can be seen to the right of his cheek (344/721/10).

Left Unlike the gunner in the previous photo, the pilot and observer of this He 111 are wearing kapok-filled life jackets which were very common among bomber crews in 1940. The significance of the scarf is not known but leads to interesting speculation. An unexpected attack of toothache seems the most likely explanation since, as neither man is wearing gloves, it cannot be uncomfortably cold in the aircraft; a mystery to which we shall never know the answer! (355/1794/12a).

Right Two 'black men' (mechanics) decorate a bomb destined for London on 13 May 1940. The legend reads 'HAPPY WHITSUN' (341/480/15a).

Aircrew of KG 2 on an airfield near Arras during the Battle of Britain plan their target routes. All are wearing the one-piece flying suit common to Luftwaffe Bomber crews in 1940 (341/481/39a).

Luftwaffe groundcrew did not have sophisticated equipment on forward airfields but still managed to keep their charges airborne. A block and tackle has been rigged on this French field to facilitate an engine change for a Bf 110 (405/556/34).

Air gunners of KG 2 clean and check their weapons. Centre figure on left-hand side is an Unteroffizer (corporal RAF, Staff Sgt USAAF) and has a mission clasp on his right breast (341/470/8).

Preparing to hand-crank a Ju 87B of 3/StG 2 (*Immelmann*) at St Malo during the Battle of Britain. Camouflage is dark green and blue and the aircraft's individual letter 'H' is painted on the starboard undercarriage spat (54/1512/27).

Above The battle damage to Ju 88 9K + FP of 6/KG 51 can be clearly seen, as can the painted-out white areas of the national markings and codes. The starboard engine has been feathered before the crash as can be seen from the position of the propeller blade. This aircraft was shot down in England (345/780/23a).

Above right All these crew members of KG 55 are wearing one-piece flying suits and in most cases brown other ranks' waist belts with Luger holster (342/603/1).

Right Crews of KG 55 take a last-minute rest beneath the wing of one of their He 111s. Three of the men are wearing kapok-filled life jackets, but the Oberfeldwebel sitting in the centre of the picture has a newer inflatable type (342/620/10a).

Left Cockpit of Ju 88A–1 of KG 51 *Eidelweiss*, showing the unit's famous badge. Aircraft is 9K + FP of the 6th Staffel, II Gruppe (345/780/24a).

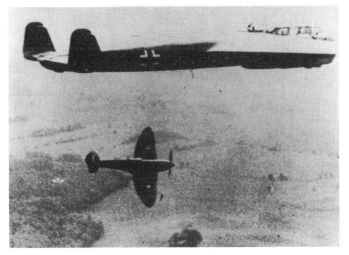

Left Having misjudged his first attack, this Spitfire pilot dives away under the Do 17 prior to pulling up and making another approach (69/94/18).

Right The uniform detail, paintwork on the Do 17 and its removed engine cowling all add interest to this picture. The Luftwaffe officer on the left is a Major and the one on the right a Leutnant. The two figures in the centre are Italian Air Force officers, the one nearest the camera being a Major; he is also wearing pilot's wings above his left pocket and medal ribbons (345/765/20).

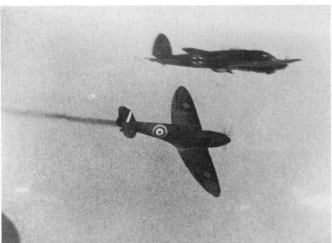

Left The more familiar position of this Spitfire in published photographs is through the front transparency of the He 111, and it is often claimed to be a fake taken for propaganda purposes. This shot neither proves nor disproves previous claims, but it does seem very likely that the Spitfire is a captured machine taking part in the making of a propaganda film (76/118/21).

Right Although these three He 111 crew members are about to embark on a Middle East raid (the map is headed Alexandria) the scene is typical of those repeated on every bomber airfield in France in 1940 (499/62/33).

Left The starboard fin of this Do 17 carries a patch over battle damage, as well as two victory bars for its gunners (342/619/25).

Left A Vauxhall auxiliary fire tender in a bombed London street, 1941 (74/136/34a).

Opposite This Unteroffizier of KG 53 is wearing an inflatable life jacket which he can be seen adjusting (**inset**), and over which he appears to be putting on a one-piece flying suit (**background photograph**). This seems to be an odd way to dress as it was customary for the life jacket to be worn over the flying suit. Aircraft is He 111 Wrk No 3714 A1 + JH of 1 Staffel, I Gruppe (342/620/6a and 8).

Below Ground equipment being used to heat the engines and interior of a Do 17Z–2 in wintry conditions in France. The weathering and dark paint daubed over the light blue undersurfaces is of interest (346/814/5).

Right Yellow and blue *Luftdienst* badge on Do 17Z of II Gruppe, Luftdienst Kommando II; small numerals below badge are 2/II (592/66/23).

Left Four crew members of a Do 17 of 9/KG 76 at Cormeilles-en-Vexin. All are wearing inflatable life jackets over their one-piece flying suits, and have their oxygen masks clipped to them (345/800/34a).

Below left Ju 88A–1 of I/KG 51 and its crew. The crewman on the left with a back pack parachute is a Leutnant, the one in the centre under the gondola is an Unteroffizier and the man on the right with the pilot-type seat parachute is a Hauptmann (402/265/3a).

Below Hermann Göring and Albert Kesselring making an informal visit to StG 77 at St Malo in 1940 (343/667/35).

Above During the Night Blitz it was not unusual to smear black paint or some other dark substance over the light blue undersides. This He 111H has a 20 mm cannon installed in the nose position. The picture may have been taken on the Eastern Front, but it illustrates typical flying gear as well as useful detail of the Heinkel's exhaust system (634/3883/1).

Above left A very pleasing shot of an He 111 of 4/KG 1 probably taken at Rosiéres-en-Santerre in 1940. The fourth Staffel badge can be clearly seen beneath the open window on which an Unteroffizier is precariously perched (385/596/5).

Left A Ju 87B of IV/LG 1 based at Pas de Calais. Gruppen I, II and III of this unit were equipped with Ju 88s which are illustrated elsewhere. The badge has a light blue background on which is a red devil astride a white bomb. This unit saw action during the Battle of Britain (383/318/10a).

Right A Hauptmann pilot of 7/III/StG 1 leaves his Ju 87B–1 (346/820/12).

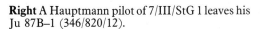

Although not a bomber, this Ju 88C–2 of 9/NJG 2 is worth including since it was developed from the original bomber design, and was used in night intruder sorties against British bomber bases as well as a straightforward night fighter. The aircraft has a 74/75/76 camouflage with odd bands around the rear fuselage. The armed guard in one photograph would appear to indicate that the crash has occurred in an occupied country (367/2377/4a, 7a and 8).

Left Under the radar. A Do 17Z, probably of 9/KG 76, hugs the wave tops as it approaches the Guernsey coast on August 27 1940 (78/21/1a).

Right Operational status board for KG 54 on July 13 1940. On that day KG 54 suffered only one casualty when one of its Ju 88s made a forced landing near Paris (403/321/32a).

Below right A Leutnant points out shipping targets in Portsmouth harbour to crews of KG 54 during July 1940 (403/325/21).

Below Geschwader Stab aircraft of KG 3 carrying the badge of the City of Elbing below its cockpit. Camouflage is dark green top surfaces and light blue under surfaces (343/679/15a).

Bottom Do 17Z–2s of KG 3 in battle formation *en route* to England in 1940 (341/456/4).

Verband	Auftrag	Start	Landg.	
		13. 7. 40.		
			7¹⁰	20 Ju 88
I/54.	Portsmouth	6⁰⁰		16 Ju 88
II/54		6⁰⁵		He 111 Seenot
K.G.54		6³⁷		He 111 "
K.G.54		7⁰⁶		

This page and top of facing page These hastily daubed badges on He 111s of KG 27 make interesting comparison with the neat Staffel and Geschwader badges which are more commonly illustrated. The messages behind some of them are obvious but others appear to be a little obscure (340/182/25a, 34a and 38a and 340/183/29 and 30).

Below Steel helmets were issued to bomber crews who often wore them in flight to give protection against gun-shot and splinter wounds. Towards the end of the war a properly designed steel helmet for use by aircrew had been issued. This gunner is an Unteroffizier and the gun is a 7·9 mm MG 15 in a Dornier Do 17 (343/699/4).

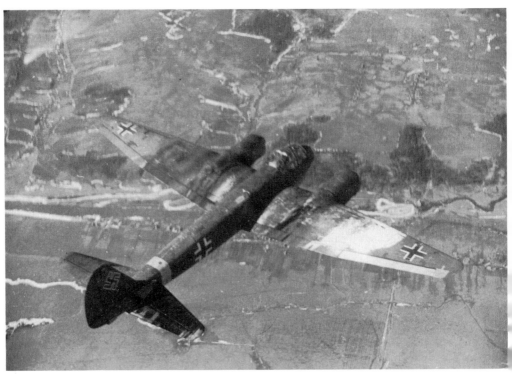

Above and left This Ju 88A–4 of an unknown unit shows just how severely paintwork could be damaged. The aircraft appears to have a new aileron on the starboard wing where there is also a large area of paint missing. The starboard tailplane is also covered in oil. Modellers who have criticised their fellows for too much weathering might care to reflect on these two photographs (632/3783/17 and 39).

Above right This air-to-air shot of a 9/KG 2 Do 17 U5 + FT makes interesting comparison with the similar view of the He 111 shown on the title page. The aircraft's individual letter, 'F', is repeated under both wing tips, a common practice on German bombers and heavy fighters (341/489/10a).

Right The MG 15 7·9 mm rear defensive armament of the Ju 87B is well shown in this view of the gunner of a StG 2 aircraft (383/319/15).

OVERLEAF

Background photograph An He 111 makes its final plunge to earth. The photograph was taken over England in 1940, but there is no record of the unit from which the aircraft came (76/99/1a).

Top inset The sinister outline of the Ju 87B is well shown by this Rotte which was photographed just after taking off for England during August 1940 (78/21/2a).

Left inset Ju 88 A–1 of Lehrgeschwader 1. These aircraft of II Gruppe operated from Orleans/Brice during 1940. Both machines show signs of having had their markings temporarily painted out at some time, and the one in the background still has its tail swastika obscured (434/574/17).

Right inset I/KG 2 airborne from Epinoy. The nearest aircraft is from the second Staffel and is coded U5 + DK (342/603/25).

Do 17Z–2 of KG 2, possibly a II Gruppe Stab aircraft, in which case full code would be U5 + AC. Band around nose is yellow (341/481/3a).

Ju 87B of II/StG 2 is bombed up. The cowling around the chin intake appears to have been renewed since the light blue paint is much cleaner than the rest of the aircraft's undersides. Top colours are the usual two shades of green 70, and 71 and the aircraft's individual letter is painted on both spats (383/313/14).

Ju 87B T6 + BC of II/StG2 (*Immelmann*). This is a Gruppe Stab aircraft and its individual code letter 'B' is in light green. Top surfaces are Dunkelgrun overall and the under surfaces are Hellblau (318/97/3a).

The FW 200 Condor was used as a long-range maritime reconnaissance aircraft, but during the Battle of Britain KG 40 operated these aircraft from Brest as long-range bombers. This is the ventral gondola and MG 151 of an FW 200C–3 (482/2874/2a).

The clean camouflage demarcation line between top and bottom colours is very evident in this view of a Geschwader Stab Do 17 5K + EA of KG 3 (345/780/14a).

Typical scene of activity around a Ju 87 of unknown unit. The cowling has been moved forward and the front half of the spinner is painted white, both of which combine to give an odd appearance to the front end of the aircraft. Small fragmentation bombs have already been loaded on the wing racks (72/85/36).

Ju 87B–1 T6 + AT of 9/StG 2 (383/301/22a).

This He 111 belonged to the 10th Staffel of IV/KG 1. This was a training Staffel used to give crews operational experience and was called the *Lehr* Staffel, 'Lehr' meaning 'learning'. Aircraft is an H–2 and has standard two-tone green and blue camouflage (385/582/6a).

Left A fully bombed-up Ju 87B of II/StG 2 sets off in the early dawn across the English Channel. The individual letter 'Z' of the photographic aircraft, possibly outlined in white, can be seen inboard of the cross (318/99/8).

Right A Kette of Ju 87Bs of II/StG 2 getting airborne from St Malo in August 1940 (318/53/35).

Below right The factory delivery call sign 'BD' can be seen either side of the underwing cross on this He 111H–2 of 7/KG 1, while the individual letter 'I' has been painted in the Staffel colour on the fuselage (white) and in black under the wing. The diamond-shaped badge on the rudder is not known (385/593/5).

Below The crew of an He 111H–2 of 10/KG 1 share a last-minute joke with their groundcrew (385/560/11).

Right A Rotte of Ju 88s. The white spinners and individual letter 'E' are very prominent and seemingly negate the whole purpose of camouflage (434/934/31).

Left Bf 110s were used as fighter-bombers against British targets. This one suffered severe damage and made a belly landing on return to its base. A salvage crew use inflatable bags and jacks to raise it back on its undercarriage (372/2600/36).

Below left A very scruffy He 111 of an unknown unit receiving some attention to its electrics under a temporary camouflaged netting cover (343/677/9).

Bottom left This is a Ju 87R–1 of II/StG 2. The Ju 87R was similar to the B but had increased range, hence the tanks on the wings of this aircraft which was photographed in the Middle East theatre but is included to enable comparisons to be made with the B versions illustrated (426/360/4).

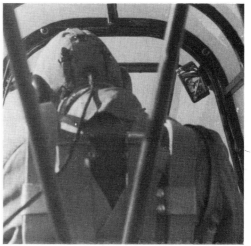

Right Gunner's view of his pilot in a Ju 87 (320/938a/6a).

Below The long glasshouse of the Ju 87B, in this case a B–2 version of IV (St) LG1. Crewmen's positions, aerial installation and details of hood slides, as well as the fit of the cowling, make useful study for modellers (320/861/20).

58

The unit identity code 1H of KG 26 can be clearly seen marked either side of the underwing cross on this He 111H–3 (320/963/17).

Despite the war the harvest must go on. Farm workers go about their normal tasks with a Do 17Z–2 of II/KG2 (*Holzhammer*) U5 + CM forming a backdrop (342/601/8).

Severe battle damage suffered by Do 17Z–2 5K + CT of 9/KG 3 during a daylight raid over England during the Battle of Britain. In view of the damage to the rear cockpit area it seems unlikely that the rear gunner escaped any form of injury. It will also be noticed that the rear tyre is flat (345/751/7 and 11).

Inset below Ju 87B of 3/StG 2 armed ready to go. The aircraft's individual letter is on the starboard spat only, a common practice in Ju 87 units, the underwing cross is well inboard and painted over the dive brakes, and the temporary wheel chocks appear to be some form of discarded containers (54/1512/3).

Above Gear down, full flap, engines on low power, an He 111 on final approach (317/40/15a).

Inset below The characteristic offset nose cone of the He 111 is shown to advantage in this view of a KG 53 aircraft being bombed-up. The fairing under the nose is the bombsight housing (344/721/10).

Above He 111H of 9/KG 53. The three bars on the starboard wing indicate III Gruppe and were used for a short period during 1940. Aircraft's code is A1 + BT (343/695/20a).

Right The pleasing lines of the He 111 are very evident in this three-quarter rear view taken from the pilot's seat of a similar aircraft (317/43/34a).

Top left Unit markings have been painted out on this He 111H–11. The dorsal turret makes interesting comparison with earlier marks, the rear end not now being exposed to the elements (461/201/5).

Centre left He 111H of KG 53 kicks up the dust as it starts its take-off run on its airfield in Belgium (342/620/31a).

Left Ju 88A–4 of 2/Kü Fl 106. The white areas in the fuselage cross have been painted out but apparently no attempt has been made to darken the Hellblau under surfaces. The individual aircraft letter 'A' is in red. The use of the tailwheel as an anchor point for the bomb loading block and tackle is of interest. (356/1805/24a).

Right Camouflaged netting forms a temporary hangar for a KG 2 Do 17 at Arras (342/602/23).

The familiar diving crow emblem can just be seen forward of the windscreen on this Ju 87B of I/StG 1. The aircraft's pristine finish would suggest that it has not long been delivered (317/30/39a).

Ju 88A–4 of KG 106. The aircraft carries simplified national markings in all positions and is probably light grey overall on its top surfaces and black underneath. Close-up detail of the wheel of another Ju 88 clearly shows the brake cable (363/2256/11a).

Do 17Z–2 of 8/KG 3 which was formed from KG 153. Under surfaces, apart from the nearest engine cowling, have had a dark colour daubed over the normal Hellblau (346/845/32).

Do 17 undercarriage detail. Comparison of the position of the mudguard in relation to the undercarriage doors on this, and other photographs of the Do 17, would indicate that this particular aircraft is well loaded and that its oleos are under full compression (344/709/28).

Above V4 + GU of 10/KG 1 over the Channel during 1940. The white squares either side of the He 111's underwing crosses are where the factory codes have been painted out (385/586/16).

Above right Do 17Z of 9/KG 76 flying over Guernsey on its way to England (78/21/5a).

Right Crew access hatch and camouflage demarcation lines, especially on the nose frames, are worth noting on this Do 17 of II/KG 3 (343/684/33a).

Left Ammunition for one of the two 7·9 mm MG 17 wing-mounted machine-guns of a Ju 87B. Weathering around the wing root and from the gun fairing to the dive brake actuator, are worthy of note by the fastidious modeller (54/1512/21).

Right The distinctive shape of the He 111 is shown to its full as this pair from I/KG 53 bank away from the camera (342/614/5).

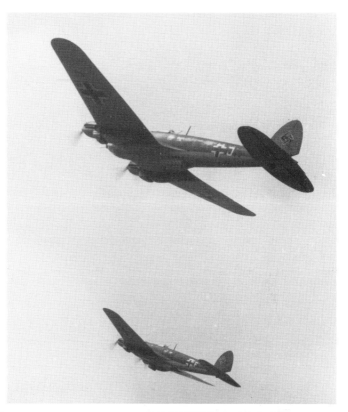

Left Bomb aimer of an He 111 at his bombsight. The steel helmet was standard issue to all Luftwaffe bomber crews. The man's kapok-filled life jacket, oxygen mask and parachute harness are all shown to advantage in this picture which has probably been posed (344/708/18).

Below Two Oberleutnants (standing), an Oberstleutnant (centre) and a Major, share a rather obvious joke about a captured RAF Ensign (343/667/30).

Left He 111 of unknown unit in early 1940 camouflage (343/694/29).

Right The Bf 110 was used as a long-range escort for the He 111s and Do 17s during the early campaigns in the Battle of Britain. It soon proved incapable of defending itself and was gradually phased out of escort duties. This aircraft of ZG 52 is typical of the Bf 110C and was taken very early in the war before its shortcomings as an escort fighter were realised. The gunner standing in the rear cockpit is a Leutnant (341/454/16).

Centre right The flat main wheel tyres and sheet draped over the nose suggest some battle damage which requires major attention, otherwise why not just jack-up the aircraft where it stands and change the wheels? The port propeller also appears to be feathered. Unit is KG 3 (342/619/29).

Bottom right He 111H–4 of KG 55. This aircraft has 70/71/65 camouflage but the underside (65) has been overpainted black. In at least one other publication a similar view of the same aircraft is captioned as being black overall, but this is clearly not so (346/846/22).

Left I/KG 53 He 111s of the first Staffel, their code letters and spinners are painted in the Staffel colour which is white (342/614/4).

Below These three He 111s have three white bars on the top surfaces of both wings as well as the rudder. Such markings were tactical and used in 1940. They usually indicated the Gruppen to which the aircraft belonged, but this was not always the case. It was more usual to see them on the top of the starboard wing only (343/694/30).

Left Kill markings on bombers are rather rare. This Do 17P of 3(F)/123, coded 4U + LL, shows a victory obtained on September 8 1939. The Staffel badge is a black anvil and hammer on a yellow background. All aircraft of this unit carried nicknames, this one was 'Lumpi', which is painted below the kill marking (340/159/5A).

Right The crew disembark from this Ju 87B of StG 5 after a successful mission. The small cross in the top corner of the fuselage cross indicates the stowage position of the first-aid equipment (346/820/10).

Below right Do 17Ps of 3(F)123 taken early in the war. These aircraft were not used against England in any quantity. The camouflage is very early three-colour 61/62/63 top surfaces and Hellblau 65 under surfaces. 4U + LL can be seen to the left (340/159/20a).

Below Maintenance work being carried out on a He 111H–2. The light area above the wing root is where the fairing has been removed. The aircraft's flaps and rear section of engine nacelle have also been taken off, as has all its armament (344/721/5).

OVERLEAF

Background photograph Do 17Z–2 F1 + KL of I/KG 76. The aircraft shows signs of a previous identity in the painted-out letter outboard of the wing cross which looks like a C (385/554/10a).

Top inset Spent cartridge cases and broken Perspex suggest that this He 111 A1 + AR of KG 53 has recently been in a fight (343/685/13).

Left inset A fitter checks the security of a small bomb on the centre rack of a Bf 110C. The aircraft belongs to III/ZG 26 and the badge is of the III Gruppe (405/585/33a).

Right inset Do 217E–4 of an unknown unit. The aircraft has two-tone grey upper surfaces and all black under surfaces, and carries simplified (outline) national markings in all positions (375/2704/6a).

Do 17s believed to be of KG 76 at Beauvais (341/475/3a).

The figures give scale to this Ju 87B of StG 77 and help one to appreciate just how large an aeroplane it was. The unit badge just below the cockpit has been practically painted out, but the rest of the aircraft seems to be in a very clean condition. The individual identity letter is on both spats on this occasion, and the small bombs under the starboard wing seem to have been dumped with gay abandon (352/1499/39).

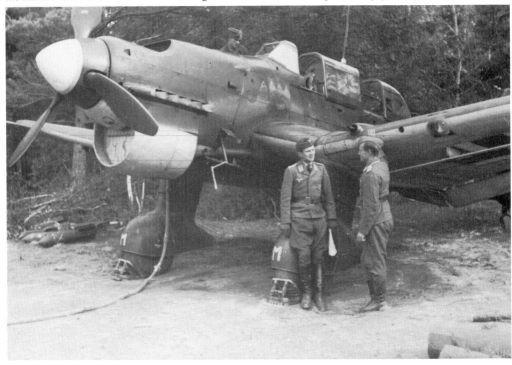

He 111H–2 of 10/KG 1 at the point of lift-off; the machine's very spindly undercarriage legs can be clearly seen (385/560/31).

A sudden gust of wind has given the armed guard on this Do 17 of I/KG 2 a rather odd-looking greatcoat. The method of picketing, and the control locks on the rudder, are both useful guides for diorama enthusiasts (345/800/28a).

Attacks against shipping in the Channel played an important part in the Luftwaffe's campaign against England. This Ju 88A–5 of KuFlGr 506 carries an LT 950 torpedo which was fitted with a wooden tail for stability during its flight; the tail broke off on impact with the water (363/2254/32a).

The pilot-operated 7·9 mm MG 15 machine-gun is very evident in this view of a Ju 88A–1 which is just about to roll (unnumbered print).

The two rear defensive machine-guns have been removed from their housings in the rear cockpit of this Ju 88A–4. The demarcation between the 70/71 top surface camouflage colours and the 65 under surface colour can be seen to have a very fine feathered edge (632/3781/36).

A candid view of factory fresh Ju 88A–1s awaiting delivery (unnumbered print).

Background photograph Pomp and ceremony was as much part of the Luftwaffe as any other air force. The significance of this particular event is unknown. Perhaps a reader can supply a logical explanation. The 'Standard' guards are both Obergefreiters (Private First Class) (536/101/27a).

Top inset Some of the He 111H aircraft in this photograph have additional armament protruding from their nose areas and under-fuselage gondolas (unnumbered print).

Bottom inset A KG 55 He 111H–16 in the spring of 1944. The top surface camouflage wraps under the wing leading edges on this particular aircraft (341/492/9).

There is a wealth of useful detail in this shot of an He 111H–16 of KG 55 taken in the spring of 1944. The bombs in the foreground are 550 lb, five of which could be carried externally on a special plate beneath the fuselage (341/492/2).

Close examination shows the centre figure to be holding a refuelling hose so it is possible these two Ju 87s are being readied for the day's work. The nearest one, unlike others illustrated in this book, does not have its identity letter on either wheel spat, but the furthest one has its on the port spat (343/691/14).

A very pleasing air-to-air shot of a Ju 87B–2 over France during 1940. The wing and fuselage bomb racks are empty. The light coloured band around the fuselage is probably some form of tactical marking (320/944/7).

He 111 of an unknown unit which came to grief in Holland. The KG identity forward of the cross has been painted out but the letters after it are CC, which indicates that it was aircraft 'C' of the Stab flight of II Gruppe. The pilot's open entry hatch and retractable windscreen, shown in the open position, tend to suggest that he used his seat in the raised position during the crash landing, maybe to ensure rapid exit when the aircraft came to rest (343/673/18).

85

Right The huge four-bladed propeller of the twin-ganged engines of the He 177 and the large wheels of the double bogie can be seen here (674/7766/35).

Left Including the photographic aircraft at least 15 Ju 87Bs can be seen in this early war shot which shows to advantage the apparent one-colour upper surfaces which are, in fact, finished in splinter pattern 70/71 (428/497/6).

Centre left He 111H G1 + LH of I/KG 55, which is probably flying on an air test as it has no signs of any armament either in the dorsal turret or gondola. Individual code, 'L', and spinners are in the Staffel colour (342/604/43).

Bottom left High hopes held for the He 177, a four-engined long-range bomber, did not materialise and the aircraft was dogged with problems throughout its operational career. This example is an A-5 version. Top surfaces are 75 and 76 and the underside is black. The aircraft's individual code letter 'S' is in white on the nose (668/7165/37a).

Below This is another KG 100 He 177, this time an A-3/R2 version used by 2/KG 100 based at Châteaudun for Operation 'Steinbock' in February 1944 (668/7165/5).

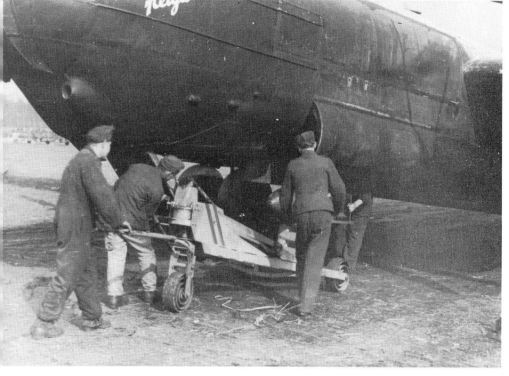

This page and top of facing page Patched and tired-looking He 177A–1s of FF(B)16 at Burg in 1944. These aircraft were all operated by KG 40 before being handed over to the training unit which was located near Magdeburg (674/7766/6, 7 and 4a).

Below How to hide your Heinkels. These examples are believed to be He 111P–2s of KG 55 in France during 1940 (405/583/27).

Left He 177A–5/R6 of II/KG 40 at Bordeaux-Merignac, 1944. At this time the unit was using its Heinkels for Atlantic reconnaissance. Camouflage is 74/75/76 (676/7969A/24).

Below left An unknown but well-decorated Stuka pilot poses before his bombed-up Ju 87B–1 somewhere in France in 1940 (343/657/38a).

Right and below Two views of an He 177A–3 of FFS(B)16 in 1944. Codes were VD + XS, badge is brown owl on white shield (674/7766/25a and 674/7766/24a).

Inset left The inverted gull wings of the Ju 87 and its angular tailplane, features impressed on all aircraft recognition classes, reflect the rather odd outline of this notorious dive-bomber (346/820/6).

Inset right This Do 17 has come to grief in a big way; the fuselage appears to be split down its centre line to the wing leading edge and the port engine ripped completely from its mounting. Unfortunately the unit and circumstances cannot be traced from the information available (343/662/9).

Background photograph One of the Luftwaffe's most famous shipping aces was Werner Baumbach, whose Ju 88A–4 is shown in this autumn 1941 picture. Shipping silhouettes on the fin/rudder have been darkened over, apart from the latest addition, and the white areas in the wing and fuselage crosses have been treated in the same way. Note also the oil streaks on the port elevator (599/1027/33).

Operational shortcomings saw the He 177 relegated to the training role. This He 177A–3, formerly operated by KG 40, is in use at an operational training school, Flugzeugführerschule (B) 16 at Burg (674/7767/7).

Grey 74 and 76 and black under surfaces are the camouflage colours for this Ju 188A–2 whose extensive nose glazing gave the crew an exceptionally good view. This machine was photographed in 1944 and possibly belonged to KG 6 (492/3340/38).

Appendix 1

The major types used by the Luftwaffe Kampf-geschwadern during their operations against England were:

Heinkel He 111
Used throughout the war the He 111 was produced in many variants and was powered by either Junkers Jumo 211D–2 or Daimler Benz DB 601A–1 engines. The crew of five were housed close together in the forward fuselage and had manually aimed defensive armament. The huge glazed nose gave the pilot a very good view but made the whole crew extremely vulnerable. Maximum bomb load was 4,410 lb which could be stored internally or externally.

Dornier Do 17
Like the He 111 the Dornier's crew were housed together, the apparent philosophy behind this being an increase in the morale level. Power was from two Bramo Fafnir 1,000 hp or two Daimler Benz 601A–1 engines. A bomb load of up to a maximum of 2,205 lb could be carried. The Do 215 was a development of the Do 17Z powered by Daimler Benz engines.

Junkers Ju 88 and 188
The Ju 88 was probably the most versatile aircraft to serve the Luftwaffe. Designed as a bomber it went on to be developed into almost every role, including night fighter, reconnaissance and intruder. Power units ranged from the Jumo 211J and 213E to the BMW 801G.

The Ju 188 was developed from the earlier aircraft and was also used in the bomber and fighter roles.

Maximum bomb load of the Ju 88 was gradually increased in the various marks to 4,410 lb, and Ju 188 carried 6,614 lb.

Ju 87B
A dive-bomber operated by Stukagesch-wadern. Its success depended a great deal on the Luftwaffe having complete air superiority. Powered by a 1,100 hp Jumo 211Da engine. Bomb load was a maximum of 3,968 lb.

Heinkel He 177
The only German four-engined bomber to see any service in strength. It was plagued by faults throughout its career and was very prone to engine fires. Power units were coupled DB 610 engines each driving one propellor and its bomb load was 13,200 lb.

Arado Ar 234
The first jet bomber to see service with any air force. Operated over England in the bomber/reconnaissance role from 1944 and used by III/KG 76 to attack vital bridges during the Allied advance after the 1944 invasion. Powered by two Junkers Jumo 004B axial turbojets. Bomb load was a maximum of 3,300 lb.

Appendix 2

The following units were active against England during the 1940 campaign.

KG 1	Staff Flight, I and II Gruppen – He 111; III Gruppe – Do 17.
KG 2	Staff Flight, I, II and III Gruppen – Do 17.
KG 3	Staff Flight, I, II and III Gruppen – Do 17.
KG 4	Staff Flight, I and II Gruppen – He 111; III Gruppe – Ju 88.
KG 26	Staff Flight, I, II and III Gruppen – He 111.
KG 27	Staff Flight, I, II and III Gruppen – He 111.
KG 30	All Ju 88.
KG 51	All Ju 88.
KG 53	All He 111.
KG 54	All Ju 88.
KG 55	All He 111.
KG 76	Staff Flight, I and III Gruppen – Do 17; II Gruppe – Ju 88.
KG 77	All Ju 88.
KG 40	All FW 200, used in reconnaissance and anti-shipping roles.
KG 126	All He 111.

KG 100	All He 111.
StG 1	ju 87.
StG 2	Ju 87.
StG 77	Ju 87.
IV (St) LG 1	Ju 87.
Stab StG 3	He 111 and Do 17.

Appendix 3

Between July 1 and October 31 1940 the Kampfgeschwadern operating against England lost the following aircraft. The figures are taken from official Luftwaffe returns and include only aircraft lost or damaged in combat, the extent of damage being taken as 60 per cent or more, which in many cases probably meant the aircraft concerned were either scrapped, used for spares, or were a long time out of action being rebuilt: *Do 215—11*;

Ju 88–273; *He 111–234*; *Do 17–196*; *Ju 87–82*; *Total – 796*.

Appendix 4

Units and their aircraft used in Operation Steinbock in 1944:

KG 2	Staff Flight, I and III Gruppen – Do 217; II Gruppe – Ju 188 V Gruppe – Me 410.
KG 6	All Ju 88.
KG 30	II Gruppe only – Ju 88.
KG 40	I Gruppe only – He 177.
KG 54	All Ju 88.
KG 66	I Gruppe only – Ju 88 and Ju 188
KG 76	Staff Flight and I Gruppe only – Ju 88.
KG 100	I Gruppe only – He 177.
SKG 10	I Gruppe only – FW 190.